CHINESE
STEP-BY-STEP
& ASIAN

Your Promise of Success

Welcome to the world of Confident Cooking,
created for you in the Test Kitchen, where
recipes are double tested by our team of
home economists to achieve a high standard
of success and delicious results every time.

CONTE

Parathas or Flaky Unleavened Bread, page 104.

Pork Chow Mein, page 48.

Scallop and Egg Flower Soup, page 22.

Crispy Fried Crab, page 27.

Balinese-style Fried Rice, page 82.

The test kitchen where our recipes are double-tested by our team of home economists to achieve a high standard of success and delicious results every time.

Spicy Potato Samosas, page 88.

The Publisher thanks the following for their assistance in the photography for this book:
Corso de' Fiori, suppliers in Sydney, NSW.

When we test our recipes, we rate them for ease of preparation. You will find the following cookery ratings on the recipes in this book, making them easy to use and understand.

A single Cooking with Confidence symbol indicates a recipe that is simple and generally quick to make – perfect for beginners.

Two symbols indicate the need for just a little more care and a little more time.

Three symbols indicate these are special dishes that need more investment in time, care and patience – but the results will be well worth it.

Pork Satays, page 74.

Rich Ice-cream with Mango, page 108.

Chinese and Asian Basics

For the authentic flavour of Chinese and Asian food, use the correct ingredients and apply the appropriate cooking techniques. Supermarkets, Asian food stores and health food shops will stock what you need.

Agar powder: Powdered agar is made from refined seaweed and is tasteless and colourless. Gives a firm set to desserts. Boil to dissolve and make it set. Use if gelatine is unavailable; however, the texture of the end product will be slightly different.

Atta flour: This very fine grade of wholemeal flour is used to make Indian breads such as chapatis. Alternatively, use plain wholemeal flour, sifting it to remove the coarse fibres.

Bamboo shoots: This crunchy, yellow vegetable is available canned and sometimes fresh. Canned shoots are either sliced or come whole in a cone shape; cut the cone into bite-sized pieces and rinse before use.

Bean pastes: There is a large range of such pastes from which to choose, varying in intensity of flavour and colours. Chilli bean paste is made of puréed soy beans, garlic and chillies. It is used in Chinese dishes to give a chilli-hot piquancy. Sweet bean paste is made from puréed soy beans, seasonings and sugar; it is used as a filling for sweet dumplings.

Bean sprouts: Available in 500 g plastic bags from fruit and vegetable shops. Look for firm, white sprouts that will have the desired sweet crunch; avoid limp, yellowish ones. Canned sprouts are also readily available; rinse them to remove the brine and soak them in iced water for about 30 minutes to improve their texture.

Agar powder · Chilli paste · Chillies · Dried chillies · Atta flour · Bamboo shoots · Coriander · Snow peas · Choi sum · Bean paste · Bok choy · Gai lum · Bean sprouts · Bean starch noodles · Black beans · Coconut milk and cream

Bean starch noodles: Fine transparent noodles are made of mung bean starch. Sold in bundles varying from 50 g to 500 g. Buy lots of small ones; it is easier than trying to divide up a large bunch. When deep-fried, these noodles swell up and become crisp. When boiled, they are slippery and are used in soups or with curry.

Black beans: Salted black beans are sold in cans and jars. Rinse them in several changes of water and mash or chop before using. Commercially prepared black bean sauce is an adequate substitute; dilute it with a little water, if necessary.

Chilli bean pastes: See Bean Pastes.

Chillies: Chillies vary in size, colour and degree of 'heat'. As a general rule, the smaller the chilli the hotter it is. Red 'bird's eye' chillies are the hottest; they are available fresh or dried. Chilli flakes are crushed, whole, dried chillies. Chilli powder is a hot seasoning spice made by grinding dried red chillies. When handling chillies, in particular fresh ones, avoid touching your eyes or face.

Chinese vegetables: Several leafy varieties (bok choy, for example) are sold at Chinese markets and some supermarkets. Buy bright green bunches with no signs of wilting. Snow peas are also often used.

Coconut milk and cream: Many brands are available; experiment until you find one of the consistency you like. If canned coconut milk or cream are not available, make your own by pouring 2½ cups very hot water over 200 g desiccated coconut. When cool enough to handle, knead and strain through a fine strainer. This will give 1½ cups coconut milk. Use hot milk to produce a very rich coconut milk.

Curry leaves: The small, glossy, green leaves are used like bay. Mostly sold dried, but also available fresh.

Dried Chinese mushrooms: While a packet of these mushrooms may seem expensive, they are used very sparingly in comparison to fresh because of their pungency. Kept in an airtight container, they will last indefinitely. Continental dried mushrooms are not a substitute, but canned straw mushrooms will provide an acceptable substitute in some recipes.

Dried lily buds: Used in specific dishes for their texture and subtle flavour. They have no substitute but may be omitted without radically altering the flavour of the dish.

Dried mandarin and tangerine peel: Look for these in Chinese grocery stores. When the fruits are in season, dry their peel in the oven for a very acceptable substitute. Even fresh orange rind will do, but use it in smaller quantities than the dried form.

Egg noodles: Sold dried in small, tangled bundles. Cook dried noodles in a large pan of rapidly boiling water, with a little oil added, until just tender. Fresh egg noodles are available in Chinese supermarkets; they need only the briefest cooking in boiling water.

Fish sauce: Sold as nuoc mam sauce. This salty, thin sauce is used in the cuisines of South East Asia in much the same way as soy sauce is used in Chinese cooking. There is no substitute for it.

Five spice powder: A common seasoning used in Chinese cooking, it tastes predominantly of star anise but also contains fennel, cinnamon, cloves and Szechuan pepper.

Fried bean curd: Found in the refrigerator section of Asian supermarkets, usually vacuum-packed or in plastic bags. You can make your own by deep-frying squares of fresh, pressed (firm) bean curd.

Dried Chinese mushrooms
Garam masala
Ghee
Dried lily buds
Lemon grass
Ginger
Dried mandarin peel
Egg noodles
Hoisin sauce
Ketchap manis
Fish sauce
Five spice powder
Galangal
Fried bean curd

Galangal: This is an aromatic ginger-like plant. Available fom Asian supermarkets, you can buy it bottled in brine or occasionally fresh. It is peeled and sliced and used in Thai soups and South East Asian recipes. Dried galangal lacks the flavour of the bottled or fresh product. It has a similar taste and texture to ginger.

Garam masala: This fragrant mix of ground spices is readily available in supermarkets. Store in an airtight container in a cool, dark place. This spice mix is used mainly in Indian cooking. It gives a much more intense and complex flavour to curries than the standard Western-style curry powders.

Ghee: Clarified butter or pure butterfat minus the water, salt and milk solids. It is available in tins and in plastic tubs in the dairy section of the supermarket. In Indian cooking, it is used for frying because it can be heated to a higher temperature than butter without burning. Also used in Indian sweet making.

Ginger: Purchase plump, fresh stems without any signs of shrivelling. Scrape or peel away the papery skin before grating or shredding. Store ginger in the vegetable crisper, or wrap it in a paper towel inside a plastic bag and refrigerate. Ground ginger is not an acceptable substitute, but bottled, grated ginger is very useful.

Hoisin sauce: A thick, red-dish-brown sauce made from soy beans, vinegar and spices. After opening, store in the refrigerator for up to six months. It has a sweet flavour and is used in cooking and as a condiment.

Ketchap manis: See Soy Sauce.

Lemon grass: This long, sturdy grass can be found in the fresh herb section at some fruit shops and supermarkets. Its distinctive white, slightly bulbous stem, is the part used. Bruise it with a heavy knife to release the flavour. Cut into short lengths for use and remove from the dish before serving. Alternatively, it can be chopped very finely and left in the dish. Substitute a few strips of lemon rind, if unavailable.

Limes and lime leaves: Limes are used in Asian dishes to add tartness. Lime leaves, particularly those of the Kaffir lime, are used for the citrus flavour they impart to the curries and fish dishes of Thailand. Fruit shops sometimes sell fresh Kaffir lime leaves; also look in Asian supermarkets. Use the very tender leaves of a lemon tree as a substitute, if necessary. Dried Kaffir lime leaves are also available; store them in an airtight container.

Mint: Mint is used in Indian cooking and is a flavour with which we are all familiar. Sometimes, however, an Asian recipe calls for Vietnamese mint, which is an entirely different species. Available only through specialty stores, it is an unusually flavoured herb, hot and peppery. Regular mint can be used, but will not give an authentic flavour.

Mustard, black: The small, dark brown seeds are very pungent. They are used in Indian cooking. Available in health food stores and Asian supermakets. They must be cooked in a dry pan until they begin to pop.

Noodles: Rice is always thought of as the staple in Asian cuisines but noodles also play their part as an important carbohydrate source in Chinese and Asian diets. The north of China is a wheat-growing area and wheat noodles are often eaten. Noodles are also made from rice flour. Rice vermicelli is commonly available in supermarkets and can be boiled, stir-fried or deep-fried. Look for a selection of dried noodles in Chinese grocery stores and also for the fresh noodles; a great array is to be found in the refrigerator section.

Oyster sauce: Readily available from supermarkets and Asian grocery stores, it is used in Chinese cooking,

especially in vegetable dishes. It is a sweetish and slightly salty, caramelly sauce. Store opened sauce in the fridge. Oyster sauce contains monosodium glutamate, a substance to which some people appear allergic, so take note.

Limes and lime leaves
Peanut oil
Pickled lime
Dried lime leaves
Short grain rice
Mint
Long grain rice
Vietnamese mint
Rice vermicelli
Black mustard seeds
Thin rice stick noodles
Egg noodles
Roti flour
Thick rice stick noodles
noodles
Saffron
Oyster sauce
Palm sugar

Palm sugar: Sold in cylinders and in hemispherical cakes, palm sugar is hard and is a very dark brown. Grate it before using. Substitute soft brown sugar, if necessary. A lighter, softer palm sugar comes in plastic canisters and is much easier to spoon out and measure. However, it does not have the right colour for all applications.

Peanut oil: A pale yellow oil with a characteristic peanut aroma and flavour that is particularly well suited to stir-fried dishes. It is very popular as a cooking oil in Asia. Store in an airtight container at room temperature.

Pickled lime: Mainly used in Indian dishes, the limes are split, filled with spices and pickled in oil.

Rice: Long-grain white rice is most commonly used in Asian cooking. Store in an airtight container in a cool, dry place. To cook by the absorption method, place rice in a pan, add enough cold water to cover rice by 3 cm; bring to the boil; boil rapidly until small tunnels appear over the surface of the rice. Reduce heat to very low, cover pan with a tight-fitting lid, cook about 10 minutes. Remove pan from heat. Leave, covered, 5 minutes before serving.

Rice vermicelli: Thin strands of rice noodles available in Asian supermarkets. They should be soaked in hot water to soften and require very little cooking. If they are to be deep-fried, do not soak; cook in moderately hot oil until they treble in size and turn very white and crisp.

Roti flour: A coarse, granular flour used for making Indian breads, it is available in health food and Asian stores. Plain white flour can be substituted.

Saffron: The world's most expensive spice, harvested from the stigmas of the crocus, it gives a subtle taste and fragrance and a golden-yellow hue to food. Purchase it as threads; they should be bright orange. (Powdered saffron is often of a lower quality.) To use, toast threads in a dry pan until crisp; cool. Crush threads with a spoon; add a little hot water to thoroughly dissolve.

Sambal oelek: A chilli purée, some-times with salt and vinegar added to preserve it. A very useful bottle to have on hand, it will keep for many months in the refrigerator. Available from supermarkets and Asian stores.

Sesame oil: A fragrant oil that features in Chinese cooking. A few drops add a sweet, nutty flavour to stir-fries and marinades. Store in the fridge once opened.

Sesame paste: Made from ground, toasted sesame seeds, it has a nutty flavour and smooth texture. Bottled tahini paste can be sub-stituted, if necessary.

Shrimp paste: The kindest thing anyone can say about the smell of this ingredient is that it is pungent. In South East Asia, it is used to en-hance the flavour of many dishes, not only those which contain seafood. Remember that a little goes a long way. It may be sold in bottles, jars or blocks and may be labelled as blachan. Once opened, wrap it very securely to seal in the odour and store in the refrigerator. Try anchovy sauce as a substitute.

Soy sauce: Light soy, the most commonly available type, is found in all super-markets. It is thin, light in colour and ideal for most stir-fried dishes when the flavour is all that is called for. Sometimes dark soy is essential when a deeper colour is required, as in slow-cooked dishes; this sauce is the heavier of the two. Shake the bottle and you will see that it runs down the inside leaving a stain on the glass. Supermarkets do not often stock this sauce, but they frequently do stock ketchap manis, a heavy, sweet soy from Indonesia. Use this if dark soy is not available, simply diluting it a little with water and reducing the sugar content of the recipe.

Spring onions: These are often sold in Australia as shallots and eschallots; in the United States they are known as scallions. Sold in bunches at the green-grocers, they are slender, green and white without a bulb at the root end.

Sambal oelek — Spring roll pastry — Star anise — Straw mushrooms — Sesame oil — Sesame paste — Tamarind pulp — Shrimp paste — Fresh water chestnuts — Soy sauce — Tinned water chestnuts — Won ton wrappers — Spring onions

Spring roll pastry: This is a very fine, white pastry, sold frozen in super-markets and Asian grocery stores. In some instances, won ton wrappers can be substituted, but these tend to cook faster than spring roll wrappers, so if the filling is raw, longer, slower cook-ing is necessary to achieve a good result. The spring roll wrappers are sold in 250 g packets, 215 mm square, containing 20 wrappers. When using spring roll pastry, always keep the sheets that you are not working on covered with a clean, damp tea-towel to prevent them from drying out. Store any unused pastry, covered securely in plastic wrap, in the freezer compartment.

Star anise: A star-shaped fruit comprised of eight seg-ments. They are sun-dried until hard and brown and have an pronounced aniseed aroma and sweet aniseed flavour. Star anise is the es-sential flavouring for Chinese five spice powder. Sold whole or ground, they will retain their flavour and aroma indefinitely in an air-tight jar. Like all spices, they must be stored in a cool place away from direct light.

Straw mushrooms: These mild-flavoured mushrooms are readily available in tins. Once opened, they will not keep for more than a few days in the refrigerator.

Tamarind: Dried tamarind pulp is used in Asian recipes for its acidic flavour. Sold as a softish cake in plastic packets, it must first be dis-solved in hot water and the liquid then strained through a sieve. Lemon juice is a good substitute.

Water chestnuts: Small, rounded, crisp vegetables, sold in tins. They give a pleasant crunchy texture to many Chinese dishes. Any unused water chestnuts will keep fresh for five days if immersed in water in the fridge; change water daily.

Won ton wrappers: Small, pliable squares of pastry made from flour and egg yolks. They are used to wrap savoury and sweet fillings that may be steamed or deep-fried. Sold fresh in packs of about 30, they can be stored in the refrigerator for up to three days.

Choosing a wok

Woks are now readily available in a variety of styles as a result of the tremendous popularity of Chinese and Asian cooking in Western countries. Woks vary in type, size and shape and in the materials used to produce them. Before selecting a wok, consider what type of stove you have. For electric stoves, consider buying a single-handed, flat-bottomed wok. This type will sit more directly and securely on the heating element, allowing a more even conduction of heat.

If you wish to free up space on the stove top, you may find an electric wok a better choice. However, because it is controlled thermostatically, the heat goes on and off and food may take longer to cook. If you plan heavy-duty work with your wok, a portable-gas wok cooker, which is attached to a gas bottle, provides great flexibility. You can cook indoors or out, and all the stove hotplates are then available for cooking other items.

Gas stoves are ideal for wok cooking. Heat is delivered instantly and is much more easily controlled than electricity. A flat-bottomed wok is a good choice. Care must be taken if choosing the traditional-style, rounded wok; a stand may be necessary to provide stability. Choose a stand that is open because this allows sufficient air to flow through, providing the best heat source. When cooking, place the ring stand over the largest burner with the narrow side up.

Woks can be made of rolled steel, stainless steel or non-stick aluminium. Rolled steel woks require seasoning before use and on-going maintenance. Some stainless steel and non-stick aluminium woks have an interior coating. Check manufacturer's instructions before removing it. These woks are easier to care for, and only require washing in hot, soapy water after use and thorough drying. Don't scrub non-stick coatings with abrasives and use only wooden cooking utensils.

Extra equipment

A domed wok lid is very useful, and enables the wok to be used for more than just stir-frying – braising and steaming are also possible. Bamboo steamer racks and a lid are ideal for cooking steamed breads and dumplings. The racks can be stacked to steam several layers at a time. For steaming items such as a whole fish, place them on a heatproof dish and then on a round cake rack which fits about two-thirds of the way up the wok and is well balanced. The boiling water is underneath and the wok lid on top.

For stir-frying, the traditional wide and flat-bladed wok charn is ideal. Wooden, charn-like spatulas are also available and are best for non-stick woks. Wooden spoons are suitable for stir-frying but avoid plastic spatulas as they tend to melt as you cook. For deep-frying, you will need a wide, slotted spoon and/or tongs to lift out the fried food. Traditional wire mesh strainers are good because the mesh allows the oil to drip away and the wooden handle does not conduct heat; therefore, your hand is protected from the intense heat.

Knives: Since so much of Asian cooking involves the preparation of the raw ingredients, it is wise to have a good quality, sharp knife to do the cutting and an hygienic, non-slip board on which to cut. Different knives have different applications. For most jobs, a Western chef's knife is the easiest to handle. If Chinese chopping a chicken or duck, a medium-weight cleaver is useful. Once you're used to the feel of it, a cleaver is a versatile implement. If preferred, a heavy-bladed chef's knife can be used.

Cooking with a wok

The wok is the utensil most closely associated with Chinese cooking and it certainly is essential for stir-frying. The sloping sides of the wok are perfect for enabling you to toss and turn the food as it cooks.

Stir-frying: This involves cooking small pieces of food over a high heat for a short amount of time. The first principle of stir-frying involves the preparation of the ingredients; the meat is often cut into even, paper-thin slices, while quick-cooking vegetables are evenly sliced or cut into small

Seasoning a wok

A rolled steel wok – the standard, inexpensive one available from Chinese and Asian stores – is coated with a thin film of lacquer to stop it rusting while on the shelf. This film has to be removed before cooking. The best way to do this is to fill the wok with cold water and to add two tablespoons of bicarbonate of soda. Bring to the boil and boil rapidly for 15 minutes. Drain, scrub off the varnish with a plastic scourer, repeating the process if any of the lacquer coating still remains.

Once this has been done, rinse and dry the wok and place it over a low heat. Make a wad with a sheet of absorbent paper and have a small bowl of cooking oil, preferably peanut oil, ready. When the wok is hot, wipe it with the absorbent paper dipped in oil, repeating the process with fresh paper until it comes away clean, without any trace of colour.

A seasoned wok should not be scrubbed. To wash the wok after cooking, use hot water and a sponge. Soak in warm water and detergent if food has stuck to it. Dry well after washing, heating it gently over a low heat and rubbing it all over with oiled, absorbent paper. Keep the wok in a dry, well-ventilated place. Long periods in a dark, warm, airless cupboard can cause the oil coating the wok to turn rancid. Using the wok frequently is the best way to prevent it rusting.

Trim meat of fat and cut across the grain into thin slices for stir-frying.

Heat wok before adding oil or meat, to sear and seal the juices.

Use a charn or wooden spoon to toss and turn the food as it cooks.

pieces. The slower-cooking vegetables are cut thinly or blanched before being added to a stir-fry. Once the slicing is done, ensure all the ingredients for the sauce are measured out and ready to be used. Keep them near the cooking area for ease of use. Have the rice or noodles cooked and ready for serving before you start to cook.

The wok itself must be hot before the oil and food are added. This ensures that the cooking time will be short and the ingredients, especially meat, will be seared instantly, sealing in the juices and flavour. Use a charn or wooden spoon to toss and turn the food carefully while it cooks. Keep the food moving constantly to ensure even

If oil temperature is correct, a bread cube will brown in it in one minute.

Remove the food with a wire mesh strainer. Drain on absorbent paper.

cooking and to prevent burning. Stir-fried vegetables should be crisp/tender, and the meat tender and succulent.

Deep-frying: The wok provides a large surface area, and makes cooking a larger amount of food possible. It provides room for foods that expand during deep-frying, such as prawn crisps and pappadams. Less oil is needed for deep-frying in a wok than in a pan because of its hemispherical shape. Safety precautions are very important when cooking with hot oil. Make sure the wok is resting securely on the stove trivets; flat-bottomed woks are good or you could use a wok ring to provide a firm base. If, even with a ring, you feel it is unstable, consider using a wide, but deep, heavy-based pan instead.

Once the pan or wok is in place, add the oil, filling it never more than half full. Heat over a high heat. Do not leave the kitchen while the oil is heating because it can quickly overheat and ignite. Watch the oil so that you know when it is hot enough to start frying. If it is the required temperature for deep-frying (180°C is appropriate), it will start to 'move', and a 3 cm cube of stale white bread will brown in it in one minute. Use a cooking thermometer to check, if necessary. Lower the heat to medium, if that is all that is needed to maintain a good cooking temperature.

Carefully add the food to the oil with tongs and move small pieces of food around, turning them to ensure even cooking. Carefully lift food out as it is done with tongs, a wire mesh strainer or a slotted spoon. Drain it on a tray covered with several layers of absorbent paper. If you have more food to deep-fry, keep the cooked food hot by placing it in a moderate 180°C

oven. Between cooking the batches of food, allow the oil to come back to its original temperature for the best results. Use a slotted spoon to remove small fragments of food that will burn as you continue to cook.

Steaming: A wok is perfect for steaming. Its sloping sides allow racks and bamboo steamers to fit firmly into place. Before you start to steam, check that you have enough – and not too much –water in your wok. If there is too much water it will boil up into the food and spoil the whole process; if there is too little it will quickly boil dry during cooking. Fill your wok about one-third full and stand the rack or steamer over the water to check the

Bamboo steamers are ideal to steam small won tons, dumplings and breads.

Whole fish are easily steamed on a serving plate placed over a wire rack.

height. Do this before you bring the water to the boil. Once boiling, arrange food over rack and carefully place in the wok. Cover wok and maintain the heat so that the water boils rapidly, allowing the steam to circulate evenly around the food as it cooks.

When lifting the lid on a wok while steaming is in progress, always lift it up and away from you like a shield so that the bare skin on your wrist is not exposed to a blast of scalding steam. Wear a long oven glove for added protection, if you wish. If your model of wok doesn't have a domed lid, a well-fitting saucepan lid or the lid of a bamboo steamer will work perfectly well.

Preparation

There is a small group of essential ingredients that appears time and time again in Chinese and Asian recipes. There are many ways to prepare them for specific cooking techniques and for decorative purposes.

Garlic: There are a great many models of garlic press on the market that will crush garlic adequately. However, the professional way to crush it is to use a sharp-bladed knife, chopping the garlic finely and working in a little salt as you go. Scrape the

Peel onions and cut into eighths or into wedges of the desired size.

Trim spring onions and slice into long, thin shreds.

Slice peeled garlic cloves into thin slices with a sharp knife.

Peel ginger and cut it crossways into thin slices with a sharp knife.

chopped garlic together into a mound. Turn it over with the knife blade and then chop it again, repeating the procedure until it is a very fine mass.

Peel onions and cut thinly and evenly into rounds.

Trim spring onions and slice into even pieces on the diagonal.

To crush garlic, use a sharp-bladed knife, working in a little salt as you go.

For shredded ginger, peel and cut lengthways into very thin strips.

Garlic can be crushed by hitting it with the flat side of a cleaver; this releases the flavour while keeping the garlic in a single mass. Sometimes more coarsely chopped garlic is required so that small, individual pieces of it can be seen. Alternatively, thin slices may be needed to flavour the cooking oil prior to adding the main ingredients.

Ginger: Sliced, minced, grated and shredded ginger are all used in Asian cooking. Again, a sharp knife is important for peeling and slicing. If the ginger is very young and fresh, it does not need to be peeled.

Slices of ginger can be covered with sherry or sake (Japanese wine) and stored in an airtight container in the refrigerator for a couple of weeks.

Onions: In the majority of instances, these are used for their texture and flavour and are chopped coarsely or finely and mixed with other ingredients in the course of cooking. However, when a more decorative look is appropriate, they can be cut into eighths or wedges of your chosen size. The layers of the onion can then be separated out if the recipe requires.

Spring onions: Used both for their flavour and their decorative qualities,

To make tamarind liquid: Dissolve pulp in hot water; separate pips. Strain.

Chillies

To prepare thin strips of chilli for decoration, use a small, sharp knife to cut the chilli in half lengthways. Remove the central membrane together with the seeds, then cut or use scissors to slice the chilli into thin strips. Whole chillies can also be sliced using scissors; hold the chilli by the stem and snip from the end. This method works well with small chillies. Avoid touching eyes or face because chilli burns.

For dried mandarin peel, remove pulp; dry in 180°C oven for 15 minutes.

spring onions can be finely chopped, sliced diagonally, sliced lengthways and also made into 'brushes'. To do this, take a piece about 7.5 cm long and make fine, parallel cuts from one end towards the centre. Place in iced water until the cuts open out, resembling a small brush.

Sometimes only the white part of the spring onion is called for in a recipe; at other times only the green or a combination of both.

Tamarind liquid: This is made from tamarind pulp, a dark brown, fibrous substance that is sold in dried form. It is used for the sour taste it lends to food. The pulp must be dissolved in hot water and the seeds separated out with your hands. The liquid is then strained and is ready for use. It can be used in marinades as a tenderising and flavouring agent and in curries and other slow-cooked dishes. It is used occasionally in stir-fries.

Dried mandarin and tangerine peel: Commonly used as a seasoning in slow-cooked dishes, dried mandarin and tangerine peel are easily prepared at home and can be stored in an air-tight jar in a cool place for months. Make up a good quantity when the fruits are in season.

Use a vegetable peeler to slice the peel thinly; cut the strips into small pieces and carefully scrape off any remaining pith or flesh. Place the pieces in a single layer on a baking tray and place in a preheated, moderate oven 180°C for 15 minutes, or until the peel has dried. Three mandarins produce about a third of a cup of peel.

Chillies: To make 'flowers' for decoration, use long, red chillies. Make five or six cuts down the length of the chilli, stopping just short of the base. Place chilli in iced water for 30 minutes or until the 'flower' opens.

Chinese-style chopped chicken

For chopping a chicken or duck Chinese-style, a medium-weight cleaver is useful. First, cut the chicken in half by cutting along the breast bone and then the backbone. Remove wings and joint drumsticks and thighs. Chop each large segment such as legs and breast into two or three depending on their size. The pieces must be a manageable size for handling with chopsticks. Use the cleaver or a heavy-bladed chef's knife by bringing it down sharply in one clean stroke. With a dense bone mass, you may need to lift the blade with the food attached to it and bring it down sharply on the board once again until food is cleanly cut.